A Giant First-Start® Reader

This easy reader contains only 58 different words,
repeated often to help the young reader develop
word recognition and interest in reading.

Basic word list for *First Day of Kindergarten*

all	hello	put
am	here	say
and	hold	says
are	hooray	school
at	I	shy
big	is	smiles
car	it's	sneakers
children	kindergarten	something
Cindy	let's	sweater
come	like	teacher
cry	look	the
day	me	this
door	Mother	today
draw	Mother's	too
first	my	tree
for	new	under
good-bye	not	walks
hall	of	will
hand	play	with
		your

First Day of Kindergarten

Written by Kim Jackson

Illustrated by Joan E. Goodman

My sneakers are new.
My sweater is, too!

Today is the first day of kindergarten.

Mother walks with me.

"Hello. Today is the first day of kindergarten!"

"Here, Cindy. Here is something for the first day of kindergarten."

"Cindy, come play with me!"

"Not today. Today is my first day of kindergarten."

It's big. My school is big!
I hold Mother's hand.

Mother smiles at me.

The hall is big!

The door is big!

My teacher is big!

"This is Cindy," says Mother.

"Hello, Cindy!"

Look at all the children.

"This is Cindy," says the teacher.

"Hello, Cindy," say the children.

I hold Mother's hand.

Mother says good-bye.

I am shy. Will I cry?

I draw.

I draw and I draw.

"Hello, Cindy. I like your tree!"

"I like your car!" I say.

I say, "Let's put your car under my tree."

"Hooray! Today is my first day of kindergarten!"